SING THE FAITH

D1562130

Hymns on

PRAYER

DAVID TRYGGESTAD

Augsburg Fortress
PUBLISHERS

Hymns on
PRAYER

DAVID TRYGGESTAD

Editors:
Vicky Goplin,
Victor Jortack,
Elizabeth Drotning
Cover design:
Marti Naughton

Scripture quotations
are from New Revised
Standard Version
Bible, copyright
© 1989 Division of
Christian Education
of the National
Council of the
Churches of Christ in
the United States of
America. Used by
permission.

Copyright © 2002
Augsburg Fortress
All rights reserved.
May not be
reproduced.
ISBN 0-8066-4428-1
Manufactured
in U.S.A.

05 04 03 02 1 2 3 4

Introduction . . . .

What A Friend We Have in Jesus . . . .

Lord, Teach Us How to Pray Aright 1

Lord Jesus Christ, We Humbly Pray 2

Stand Up, Stand Up For Jesus 3

Love Divine, All Loves Excelling 3

Resources 4

INTRODUCTION

Welcome to Sing the Faith!

Welcome to *Hymns on Prayer,* one of three volumes in the Sing the Faith Bible Study series. You are embarking on a biblical exploration of grace through the poetry, music, and history of five of the most beloved hymns of the Christian tradition.

Hymns are the faith people sing. The lyrics are owned by the people as the fabric of their theology. Many hymns have been in the memories of churchgoers for years. The melodies and texts of hymns are often retained after most other memory has faded. This series will allow participants to connect these well-loved hymns to biblical texts.

Pastors and worship leaders spend a significant amount of time searching for hymns related to the Sunday readings, the theme, and the mood of each service. Indexes are available to assist planners in coordinating biblical texts and songs. The Sing the Faith series brings this information and its powerful faith formation capability to you.

Each session focuses on one hymn. Participants will reflect on their personal history with the hymn, explore biblical connections in the texts, learn the history and legends associated with the hymn, and consider how the message of the hymn applies to their daily journey of faith.

Preparing your study

The Sing the Faith series, designed for small-group Bible study, encourages interaction among participants to help them grow and enrich their journeys of faith. Alternate groupings, with minor modifications, would be possible. Individuals might use this resource for personal study or partner with another individual to study and correspond by phone or e-mail.

The thematically connected hymns in each volume can be studied at any time and in any church season. The five-week structure makes this an ideal choice during the season of Lent.

The material is planned for weekly gatherings. The meeting place could be at church or in homes. The key will be finding a place where everyone can feel safe as they share, reflect, and pray together.

This study is ideal for rotational leadership. As leaders and participants discover increased connection between worship and study, the understanding of leadership will continue to broaden. If a pastor is a part of your group, include him or her in the rotation. The opportunity to operate as a participant will be welcomed.

Adults of all ages and stages will find this study useful—singles groups, men's breakfasts, mom's time out, and new member study are just a few ideas. Because of the universality of the hymns used in this series, a young adult group may be as vital as an older adult group.

Planning each session

Gathering for the story

The first three pages of each session introduce the hymn. The instructions invite you to transition from a time of fellowship as you arrive, to gathering your thoughts about the hymn, checking in with each other, and then experiencing the hymn (see page 6), and finally prayer together.

Learning the story

This section provides relevant information about the text, the tune, and the legends of each hymn. The intent is not in-depth study, but an opportunity to discover stories and anecdotes about the persons and circumstances that were a part of the creation of the hymn.

Our story

Hymns and songs carry emotional and cognitive memories. In this section you will be asked to reflect on how the hymn has been part of your growth in the Christian faith. The questions, similar in all sessions, provide time and a safe opportunity to share how the music and poetry has affected who we are as believers.

The biblical story

Unless the hymn writer indicated a specific biblical passage, the intended textual connection can never be certain. The writer of this study discovered textual connections and images for one stanza of each hymn and has provided questions to help you search for personal meaning related to faith traditions and the Bible.

Texts were selected from the New Revised Standard Version of the Bible (NRSV), but each participant may use his or her own Bible. Using a variety of translations can bring new perspectives to your discussions.

Additional questions to reflect on in this section of the study are:

◆ What is normally taken for granted about this passage?

◆ What is related to your own journey of faith?

◆ What connections to biblical and doctrinal understanding do you find?

◆ What may affect you personally in this text?

Living the story

Each hymn ends with three questions addressing how this hymn will affect the way you live your faith as a result of your learning. What message will you bring to each day?

Each session ends with praying and singing. The closing prayer, with time for individual petitions, and singing weave new dimensions to the hymn's familiar words and images.

Experiencing the hymn

An important part of this study is the experience of singing. Whether you group is large or small, raise your voices together each week. If a piano and accompanist are available, look for the full score in your favorite hymnal. All hymns are included in *Lutheran Book of Worship* or *With One Voice*, as well as in most traditional Christian hymnals.

If your group has instrumentalists, invite them to play with you as you sing. Perhaps someone's hidden talent will shine! Invite a young person or two from your congregation who play in their school orchestra or band to play along for one session.

Many of the hymns in the Sing the Faith volumes appear on numerous recordings. The reference list on page 47 offers a starting place for your search. You might publicize your study in your church newsletter or bulletin by listing the hymns and asking for recording recommendations. In addition, piano collections that include one or more of the hymns are suggested on this page.

Whether you sing *a cappella* or with a pipe organ at its fullest, enjoy your time with the music, with the texts, with memories of the past and hope for the future, and with each other as together you Sing the Faith.

WHAT A FRIEND WE HAVE IN JESUS

1 What a friend we have in Je - sus, all our sins and griefs to bear!
2 Have we tri - als and temp-ta - tions? Is there trou-ble an - y - where?
3 Are we weak and heav - y - lad - en, cum-bered with a load of care?

What a priv - i - lege to car - ry ev - 'ry-thing to God in prayer!
We should nev - er be dis - cour - aged— take it to the Lord in prayer.
Pre - cious Sav - ior, still our ref - uge— take it to the Lord in prayer.

Oh, what peace we of - ten for - feit; oh, what need-less pain we bear—
Can we find a friend so faith - ful who will all our sor-rows share?
Do your friends de-spise, for - sake you? Take it to the Lord in prayer.

all be - cause we do not car - ry ev - 'ry-thing to God in prayer!
Je - sus knows our ev - 'ry weak - ness— take it to the Lord in prayer.
In his arms he'll take and shield you; you will find a so - lace there.

Text: Joseph Scriven, 1820–1886
Music: CONVERSE, Charles C. Converse, 1832–1918

GATHERING FOR THE STORY

Greet participants as they arrive. Invite them to record their responses to these questions. If possible, choose a space for this meeting that is visually inviting.

Begin with introductions. Ask volunteers to share their images of God, then say the prayer together.

Invite participants to sing "What a Friend We Have in Jesus" (see page 6).

(10 minutes)

When I was growing up, my image of God was

Now my image of God is need for him + his care for me family + friends. Having a daily

Lord Jesus, we come before you with all our cares.
You know our sins and griefs,
    and you come to us as our friend,
    a friend who can bear our griefs and sorrows.
Help us in all circumstances of our lives
    to turn to you to receive the peace
    only you can give.
In your holy name we pray.
Amen

WHAT A FRIEND WE HAVE IN JESUS

What a friend we have in Jesus,
all our sins and griefs to bear!
What a privilege to carry
ev'rything to God in prayer!
Oh, what peace we often forfeit;
oh, what needless pain we bear—
all because we do not carry
ev'rything to God in prayer!

Have we trials and temptations?
Is there trouble anywhere?
We should never be discouraged—
take it to the Lord in prayer.
Can we find a friend so faithful
who will all our sorrows share?
Jesus knows our ev'ry weakness—
take it to the Lord in prayer.

Are we weak and heavy-laden,
cumbered with a load of care?
Precious Savior, still our refuge—
take it to the Lord in prayer.
Do your friends despise, forsake you?
Take it to the Lord in prayer.
In his arms he'll take and shield you;
you will find a solace there.

Text: Joseph Scriven, 1820-1886

LEARNING THE STORY

After participants read the hymn background, talk about information that was meaningful or inspiring. (5 minutes)

The hymn

This text could only have been written by one acquainted with grief. Joseph Scriven, known as "the man who saws wood for poor widows and sick people who are unable to pay," was born in Ireland in 1819. He emigrated to Canada after his fiancée accidentally drowned on the eve of their wedding. Tragedy struck a second time when a brief illness took the life of another fiancée. As a member of the Plymouth Brethren, he lived a life of poverty and Christian service, working with the poor and the sick. Plagued by ill health and depression, he too drowned in 1886.

In 1855 Scriven wrote this text to comfort his sorrowing mother in Ireland. When asked about its origin, he replied, "The Lord and I did it between us." In 1865 "What a Friend We Have in Jesus" was published in *Social Hymns, Original and Selected* by Horace Hastings in Boston.

The tune

CONVERSE is named after its composer, Charles Converse, who was born in Massachusetts in 1832. After studying law, philosophy, and music in Leipzig, Germany, where he became acquainted with Franz Liszt, he practiced law in Erie, Pennsylvania. While he declined the offer of a Doctor of Music degree from Cambridge University, he was awarded a Doctor of Laws degree from Rutherford College in 1895. He died in 1918. The tune, also known as FRIENDSHIP, was published in 1870 in *Silver Wings* under Converse's pseudonym, Karl Reden.

OUR STORY

When did you hear this hymn for the first time?

You may need to adapt these questions for the participants in your group. Ask them to record their responses and then share their stories. *(10 minutes)*

What personal memories do you associate with this hymn?

Have there been times in your life when this hymn has been more meaningful to you than others?

THE BIBLICAL STORY

Invite participants to find the passages in their Bibles and record their responses to the questions.

What a friend we have in Jesus
John 15:12-15

What are words you use to describe a friend?

How do these words apply when you think of Jesus as your friend?

All our sins and griefs to bear!
Isaiah 53:3-6

What relief or release have you experienced as a result of turning your sins and griefs over to Jesus?

Our hymn is about Jesus; yet we are invited to take ev'rything to *God* in prayer.

Ev'rything to God in prayer!
John 10:30

Do you think of God and Jesus in the same way Why or why not? How does this text inform your thinking?

Oh, what peace we often forfeit
John 14:27

How do you define peace?

Determine if your group would prefer to:
◆ read and respond to all passages and questions before talking

◆ read, respond, and discuss one passage at a time
(20 minutes)

When have you experienced true peace even in the midst of great sorrow or pain?

In his arms he'll take and shield you
John 10:27-28

Can you think of circumstances when you felt held in the arms of Jesus? Describe this experience.

LIVING THE STORY

Invite participants to reflect for a few moments on today's conversation, then respond to the questions. It is important to share responses to these questions so your group can offer prayer support for each other throughout the next week.

Select a leader for your next gathering and remind everyone of the time and location.

Sing or listen to "What a Friend We Have in Jesus" one more time. Invite the group to pray together.

(10 minutes)

What is the message of this hymn for you?

How can you apply this message to your life?

How does this hymn speak to your prayer life?

Lord Jesus, precious Savior, refuge, faithful friend.
Thank you for the privilege
    to carry everything to you in prayer.
Thank you for speaking to us
    through this beloved hymn and this study.
Take us and shield us in your arms.
Listen now to the hearts and minds of your people.
Silence for reflection.
In your precious name we pray. Amen

LORD, TEACH US HOW TO PRAY ARIGHT

1 Lord, teach us how to pray a - right, with rev - 'rence and with fear.
2 We per - ish if we cease from prayer; oh, grant us pow'r to pray.
3 Give deep hu - mil - i - ty; the sense of god - ly sor - row give;
4 Faith in the on - ly sac - ri - fice that can for sin a - tone;
5 Give these, and then your will be done; thus strength-ened with all might,

Though dust and ash - es in your sight, we may, we must draw near.
And when to meet you we pre - pare, Lord, meet us on our way.
a strong de - sire, with con - fi - dence, to hear your voice and live;
to cast our hopes, to fix our eyes on Christ, on Christ a - lone.
we, through your Spir - it and your Son, shall pray, and pray a - right.

Text: James Montgomery, 1771–1854, alt.
Music: SONG 67, Orlando Gibbons, 1583–1625

GATHERING FOR THE STORY

Greet participants as they arrive. Invite them to record their responses to these questions in their books.

Be sure participants remember each others' names. Ask volunteers to share their images of prayer, then pray together.

Invite participants to sing "Lord, Teach Us How to Pray Aright" (see page 6).

(10 minutes)

While I was growing up, my idea of prayer was

As I have gotten older, my ideas about prayer have changed in these ways:

Lord Jesus, you taught your disciples to pray;
  teach us too.
Create in us a right spirit,
  a spirit of reverence and holy fear.
Lord, without you we perish;
  meet us today in this study.
We cast our hopes and fix our eyes
  on you alone, O Lord.
In your holy name we pray. Amen

LORD, TEACH US HOW TO PRAY ARIGHT

Lord, teach us how to pray aright,
with rev'rence and with fear.
Though dust and ashes in your sight,
we may, we must draw near.

We perish if we cease from prayer;
oh, grant us pow'r to pray.
And when to meet you we prepare,
Lord, meet us on our way.

Give deep humility; the sense
of godly sorrow give;
a strong desire, with confidence,
to hear your voice and live;

Faith in the only sacrifice
that can for sin atone;
to cast our hopes, to fix our eyes
on Christ, on Christ alone.

Give these, and then your will be done;
thus strengthened with all might,
we, through your Spirit and your Son,
shall pray, and pray aright.

Text: James Montgomery, 1771-1854, alt.

LEARNING THE STORY

After participants read the hymn background, talk about information that was meaningful or inspiring.
(5 minutes)

The hymn

James Montgomery, born in Scotland in 1771, wrote this hymn in 1818 for the Sunday school in Sheffield. His parents, who died as missionaries in the West Indies, intended for him to be a Moravian minister, but his love of poetry led him into a literary career. As the publisher of *The Sheffield Iris*, a radical political newspaper, he was imprisoned twice for articles exposing him as an outspoken critic of slavery. From his experiences, Montgomery wrote a collection of poems, *Prison Amusements*.

He was one of the most prolific contributors to English hymnody, including "Angels from the Realms of Glory." "Lord, Teach Us How to Pray Aright" was published in Thomas Cotterill's *Selection of Psalms and Hymns for Public Worship* and Edward Bickersteth's *Treatise on Prayer*.

The tune

One of the most important collections of English hymnody of the seventeenth century was George Wither's *The Hymnes and Songs of the Church*, 1623. The tunes were prepared by Orlando Gibbons (1583-1625), a significant composer of English church music. This collection was controversial in its day because some of the texts were not based on Psalms. Ralph Vaughan Williams discovered this largely forgotten collection and introduced these fine tunes in *The English Hymnal* (1906). The tune, SONG 67, has carried several different texts, the first being Psalm 1 in E. Prys's *Llyfr y Psalmau* in 1621.

OUR STORY

What do you remember about the first time you heard this hymn?

You may need to adapt these questions for the participants in your group. Ask them to record their responses and then share their stories. *(10 minutes)*

What personal memories do you associate with this hymn?

What does this hymn say to you?

THE BIBLICAL STORY

Invite participants to find the passages in their Bibles and record their responses to the questions.

Lord, teach us how to pray aright
Luke 11:1-4

Who taught you how to pray? Describe the prayer posture or patterns you were first taught.

What is your first memory of the Lord's Prayer?

With rev'rence and with fear
Psalm 89:7

Is it possible to pray irreverently?

In this context, what does fear *mean? Is it a helpful word?*

We may, we must draw near
Exodus 3:1-6

Are there boundaries between God and you? When in your life have you felt closest to God?

How does prayer draw you nearer to God? How does it invite God to draw near to you?

Determine if your group would prefer to:
◆ read and respond to all passages and questions before talking
◆ read, respond, and discuss one passage at a time
(20 minutes)

We perish if we cease from prayer
Isaiah 50:4
John 4:10-15

Have you felt like perishing for lack of the power of God in your life? How did you learn to listen for God?

To hear your voice and live
John 10:1-5

Describe circumstances when you heard the voice of Jesus. How did you feel supported?

LIVING THE STORY

Invite participants to reflect for a few moments on today's conversation, and then respond to the questions. It is important to share responses to these questions so your group can offer prayer support for each other through-out the next week.

Select a leader for your next gathering and remind every-one of the time and location.

Sing or listen to "Lord, Teach Us How to Pray Aright" one last time. Invite the group to pray together.

What does this hymn say to you at this time in your life?

How does it affect the way you live each day?

How does this hymn speak to your prayer life?

Lord, we thank you for teaching us how to pray.
Put in us a strong desire to hear your voice and live.
We pray that your will would be done in our lives.
We ask you now to listen
    to the hearts and minds of your people.
Silence for reflection.
We pray in the confidence that we,
    through your Spirit and your Son,
        shall pray, and pray aright.
Amen

LORD JESUS CHRIST, WE HUMBLY PRAY

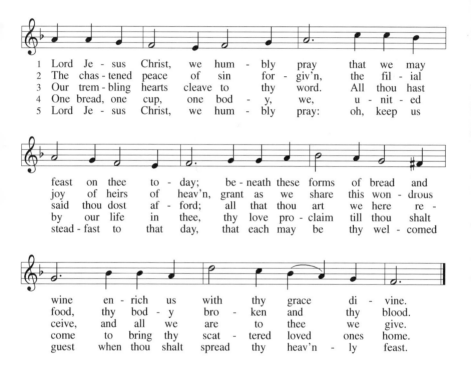

1 Lord Je - sus Christ, we hum - bly pray that we may
2 The chas - tened peace of sin for - giv'n, the fil - ial
3 Our trem - bling hearts cleave to thy word. All thou hast
4 One bread, one cup, one bod - y, we, u - nit - ed
5 Lord Je - sus Christ, we hum - bly pray: oh, keep us

feast on thee to - day; be - neath these forms of bread and
joy of heirs of heav'n, grant as we share this won - drous
said thou dost af - ford; all that thou art we here re -
by our life in thee, thy love pro - claim till thou shalt
stead - fast to that day, that each may be thy wel - comed

wine en - rich us with thy grace di - vine.
food, thy bod - y bro - ken and thy blood.
ceive, and all we are to thee we give.
come to bring thy scat - tered loved ones home.
guest when thou shalt spread thy heav'n - ly feast.

Text: Henry E. Jacobs, 1844–1932
Music: GRACE CHURCH, Ignaz J. Pleyel, 1757–1831

Greet participants as they arrive and invite them to record their responses to these questions in their books. Consider a dinner party plan for this hymn. Enjoy preparing a feast together or ask participants to bring their favorite dishes.

Ask volunteers to share words and phrases from their responses, and then say the prayer together.

Invite participants to sing "Lord Jesus Christ, We Humbly Pray" (see page 6). This hymn is especially beautiful when sung in four-part harmony. It is important to encourage the entire group to sing.

When I think of the Lord's Supper, some words or phrases that come to mind are

forgiving if sin
Celebrate
Eat & drink

When I think of a feast, some words or phrases that come to mind are

Lord Jesus Christ, we humbly pray
    for your presence with us here.
As you revealed yourself to the disciples
    in the breaking of bread,
So now reveal yourself to us
    as we sing and study your word.
Empower us with your Spirit
    to see and know you more fully.
In your holy name we pray. Amen

LORD JESUS CHRIST, WE HUMBLY PRAY

Lord Jesus Christ, we humbly pray
that we may feast on thee today;
beneath these forms of bread and wine
enrich us with thy grace divine.

The chastened peace of sin forgiv'n,
the filial joy of heirs of heav'n,
grant as we share this wondrous food,
thy body broken and thy blood.

Our trembling hearts cleave to thy word.
All thou hast said thou dost afford;
all that thou art we here receive,
and all we are to thee we give.

One bread, one cup, one body, we,
united by our life in thee,
thy love proclaim till thou shalt come
to bring thy scattered loved ones home.

Lord Jesus Christ, we humbly pray:
oh, keep us steadfast to that day,
that each may be thy welcomed guest
when thou shalt spread thy heav'nly feast.

Text: Henry E. Jacobs, 1844-1932

LEARNING THE STORY

After participants read the hymn background, talk about information they found meaningful or inspiring.
(5 minutes)

The hymn

Hymn writer Henry E. Jacobs was the grandfather of Edward T. Horn III and Henry E. Horn, both important contributors to the *Service Book and Hymnal* (1958). He was born in 1844 and attended college and seminary in his hometown of Gettysburg, Pennsylvania. His father, a pastor and scientist, owned the only telescope in the county and used it to show Union soldiers the terrain before the Battle of Gettysburg. Jacobs' witnessing of the bloody battle and caring for the wounded left an indelible imprint on him.

After serving as pastor in Pittsburgh and Philipsburg, Pennsylvania, Jacobs served as a teacher, scholar, and author, most notably at the Evangelical Lutheran Seminary at Philadelphia. He died in 1932. This hymn, written in 1910, came to be included in *The Common Service Book* (1917) during the time of another great war.

The tune

The composer of the tune GRACE CHURCH, Ignaz Pleyel, was also familiar with war. The French Revolution interrupted his tenure as director of music at the Strasbourg Cathedral. Born in 1757, the twenty-fourth child of a schoolmaster in a village near Vienna, Pleyel studied music with Franz Joseph Haydn. As a conductor, he was a familiar face to London concertgoers in the 1790s. Ending his career in Paris, he became a music publisher and established the piano factory that bore his name. He died in 1831. The tune GRACE CHURCH was published by William Gardiner in *Sacred Melodies* (1815).

OUR STORY

What do you remember about the first time you heard this hymn?

What personal memories do you associate with this hymn?

What does this hymn say to you?

You may need to adapt these questions for the participants in your group. Ask them to record their responses and then share their stories. *(10 minutes)*

THE BIBLICAL STORY

Invite participants to find the passages in their Bibles and record their responses to the questions.

Messiah, Lord, and *Christ* are titles, not names.

Lord Jesus Christ
Mark 8:27-30
Acts 10:36

What do these titles mean for you? What is similar or dissimilar about each title?

We humbly pray
Micah 6:8

What does it mean to walk humbly with your God?

What does it mean to pray humbly?

These words were scandalous to most of those who first heard them.

Feast on thee
John 6:48-59

How do you react?

Is prayer a way of feasting on Jesus?

Beneath these forms of bread and wine

1 Corinthians 11:23-26

How do you experience Christ's presence in the Lord's Supper? Is it different from other experiences of Christ in your life?

Lutheran doctrine asserts Christ is truly present in, with, and under the forms of bread and wine.

Our trembling hearts cleave to thy Word

Luke 24:13-32

In what circumstances has your heart ever trembled or burned within you at hearing the Word of God?

Determine if your group would prefer to:
◆ read and respond to all passages and questions before talking
◆ read, respond, and discuss one passage at a time
(20 minutes)

One bread, one cup, one body

1 Corinthians 12:12-13, 26-27

How can the Lord's Supper feel like individual communion with God and a communal event?

LIVING THE STORY

Invite participants to reflect for a few moments on today's conversation, and then respond to the questions. It is important to share responses to these questions so your group can offer prayer support for each other throughout the next week.

Select a leader for your next gathering and remind everyone of the time and location.

Sing or listen to "Lord, Lord Jesus Christ, We Humbly Pray" one last time. Invite the group to pray together.

What does this hymn say to you at this time in your life?

How does it affect the way you live each day?

How does this hymn speak to your prayer life?

Lord Jesus Christ, we humbly pray,
   be with us this and every day.
Thank you for this hymn and for this study.
Listen now to the hearts and minds of your people.
Silence for reflection.
Keep us steadfast in your Word
   until we see you face to face,
   guests at your heavenly feast.
In your holy name we pray. Amen

STAND UP, STAND UP FOR JESUS

1 Stand up, stand up for Je - sus, as sol - diers of the cross,
2 Stand up, stand up for Je - sus; the trum - pet call o - bey;
3 Stand up, stand up for Je - sus, stand in his strength a - lone;
4 Stand up, stand up for Je - sus, the strife will not be long;

lift high his roy - al ban - ner; it must not suf - fer loss.
stand forth in might - y con - flict in this his glo - rious day.
the arm of flesh will fail you, you dare not trust your own.
this day the din of bat - tle, the next the vic - tor's song.

From vic - t'ry un - to vic - t'ry his ar - my he shall lead,
Let all his faith - ful serve him a - gainst un - num - bered foes;
Put on the gos - pel ar - mor; each piece put on with prayer.
The sol - diers, o - ver - com - ing, their crown of life shall see,

till ev - 'ry foe is van - quished and Christ is Lord in - deed.
let cour - age rise with dan - ger, and strength to strength op - pose.
Where du - ty calls or dan - ger, be nev - er want - ing there.
and with the King of glo - ry shall reign e - ter - nal - ly.

Text: George Duffield, 1818–1888, alt.
Music: WEBB, George J. Webb, 1803–1887

GATHERING FOR THE STORY

Greet participants as they arrive. Invite them to record their responses to these questions in their books.

Ask volunteers to share words and phrases from their responses, and then say the prayer together.

Invite participants to sing "Stand Up, Stand Up for Jesus" (see page 6). It is important to encourage the entire group to sing.

What images come to mind in the phrase soldier of the cross?

When I think of Gospel armor, I think of the following:

Lord Jesus, clothe us with your gospel armor.
As you have stood up for us in our place,
suffering on our behalf,
so help us to stand up for you.
Help us to stand in your strength alone.
Be with us in our study today,
that we may be empowered
to be effective soldiers of the cross.
Amen

STAND UP, STAND UP FOR JESUS

Stand up, stand up for Jesus, as soldiers of the cross,
  lift high his royal banner; it must not suffer loss.
  From vict'ry unto vict'ry his army he shall lead,
  till ev'ry foe is vanquished and Christ is Lord indeed.

Stand up, stand up for Jesus; the trumpet call obey;
  stand forth in mighty conflict in this his glorious day.
  Let all his faithful serve him against unnumbered foes;
  et courage rise with danger, and strength to strength oppose.

Stand up, stand up for Jesus, stand in his strength alone;
  ʒe arm of flesh will fail you, you dare not trust your own.
  Put on the gospel armor; each piece put on with prayer.
  Where duty calls or danger, be never wanting there.

Stand up, stand up for Jesus, the strife will not be long;
  this day the din of battle, the next the victor's song.
  The soldiers, overcoming, their crown of life shall see,
  and with the King of glory shall reign eternally.

Text: George Duffield, 1818-1888, alt.

LEARNING THE STORY

After participants read the hymn background, talk about information they found meaningful or inspiring.
(5 minutes)

The hymn

George Duffield, Jr. was born in Pennsylvania in 1818, graduated from Yale College and Union Theological Seminary, and became a Presbyterian minister. He served congregations in New York, New Jersey, Pennsylvania, Illinois, and Michigan. This hymn was inspired by a sermon entitled "Stand up for Jesus" preached by Dudley Tyng at a YMCA gathering in 1858 during the great revival. On the following Wednesday, Tyng's arm was torn away in a farming accident. As he lay dying, Tyng's message to the people was, "Let them all stand up for Jesus." Duffield penned the hymn for worship the next Sunday. It became instantly popular, especially among soldiers in the Civil War, and was published in 1868 in *Lyra Sacra Americana*. Duffield, whose son Samuel was a noted author and historian of hymnody, died 1888 in New Jersey.

The tune

WEBB, named after its composer, George J. Webb, was first associated with a secular text, "'Tis dawn, the lark is singing." Born in England in 1803 to a successful farming family, Webb chose music over ministry for a career. After emigrating to Boston in 1830 he became organist at Old South Church and remained in that position for 40 years. He was also professor at the Boston Academy of Music and president of the Handel and Haydn Society. He died in New Jersey in 1887. Webb was first published in 1837 in *The Odeon: A Collection of Secular Melodies*, a collaborative effort by Webb and Lowell Mason.

OUR STORY

Describe the style or mood of this hymn tune as you have experienced it.

You may need to adapt these questions for the participants in your group. Ask them to record their responses and then share their stories. (10 minutes)

Does that contrast with how you would imagine the style or mood for the original secular text, "'Tis dawn, the lark is singing"?

What does this hymn say to you about strength?

THE BIBLICAL STORY

Invite participants to find the passages in their Bibles and record their responses to the questions.

Soldiers of the cross
2 Timothy 2:1-7

What do soldiers, athletes, and farmers have in common?

In what ways do you think of yourself as a soldier of the cross?

To gird your belt of truth breastplate of righteousness shoes that will guide you toward peace. Helmet of salvation. Sward of the spirit

Till ev'ry foe is vanquished. . .
against unnumbered foes
Ephesians 6:10-12

When have you come up against unnumbered foes?

The trumpet call obey
Joshua 6:1-5

Is prayer like listening to a trumpet call or a sti small voice?

The arm of flesh will fail you
2 Corinthians 12:7b-10

Do you feel the power of God most profoundly in your triumphs or in your failings?

When and how has God's grace been sufficient for you?

Determine if your group would prefer to:
♦ read and respond to all passages and questions before talking
♦ read, respond, and discuss one passage at a time
(20 minutes)

Put on the Gospel armor
Ephesians 6:13-17

Imagine yourself wearing this armor. Do you feel encumbered or empowered? What contemporary images of gospel armor can you envision?

Each piece put on with prayer
Ephesians 6:18

Do you view daily prayer as a way to arm yourself for each day?

LIVING THE STORY

Invite participants to reflect for a few moments on today's conversation, and then respond to the questions. It is important to share responses to these questions so your group can offer prayer support for each other throughout the next week.

Select a leader for your next gathering and remind everyone of the time and location.

Sing or listen to "Stand Up, Stand Up for Jesus" one last time. Invite the group to pray together.

What does this hymn say to you at this time in your life?

How does it affect the way you live each day?

How does this hymn speak to your prayer life?

Lord Jesus, we stand in your strength alone.
Our arms of flesh will fail us;
we dare not trust our own.
Empower us with the gospel armor;
clothe us with your love.
Listen now to the hearts and minds of your people.
Silence for reflection.
In your holy name we pray. Amen

LOVE DIVINE, ALL LOVES EXCELLING

1 Love di - vine, all loves ex - cel - ling, Joy of
2 Breathe, oh, breathe thy lov - ing Spir - it in - to
3 Come, Al - might - y, to de - liv - er; let us
4 Fin - ish then thy new cre - a - tion, pure and

heav'n, to earth come down! Fix in us thy
ev - 'ry trou - bled breast; let us all in
all thy life re - ceive; sud - den - ly re -
spot - less let us be; let us see thy

hum - ble dwell - ing, all thy faith - ful mer - cies crown.
thee in - her - it; let us find thy prom - ised rest.
turn, and nev - er, nev - er - more thy tem - ples leave.
great sal - va - tion per - fect - ly re - stored in thee!

Je - sus, thou art all com - pas - sion, pure, un -
Take a - way the love of sin - ning; Al - pha
Thee we would be al - ways bless - ing, serve thee
Changed from glo - ry in - to glo - ry, till in

bound - ed love thou art; vis - it us with
and O - me - ga be; end of faith, as
as thy hosts a - bove, pray, and praise thee
heav'n we take our place, till we cast our

thy sal - va - tion, en - ter ev - 'ry trem - bling heart.
its be - gin - ning, set our hearts at lib - er - ty.
with - out ceas - ing, glo - ry in thy per - fect love.
crowns be - fore thee, lost in won - der, love, and praise!

Text: Charles Wesley, 1707–1788
Music: HYFRYDOL, Rowland H. Prichard, 1811–1887

Gathering for the Story

Greet participants as they arrive and invite them to record their responses to these questions.

Ask volunteers to share words and phrases from their responses, and then say the prayer together.

Invite participants to sing "Love Divine, All Loves Excelling" (see page 6). This hymn is especially beautiful when sung in four-part harmony.

How do you interpret temple of the Lord?

When I think of praying without ceasing, I think:

Love divine, all loves excelling, be with us.
Joy of heav'n, to earth come down.
Come, Almighty, to deliver;
    let us all thy life receive.
Make of our hearts your holy temple.
Inhabit the praises of your people
    as we sing our song today.
In your holy name we pray. Amen

LOVE DIVINE, ALL LOVES EXCELLING

Love divine, all loves excelling, Joy of heav'n, to earth come down!
Fix in us thy humble dwelling, all thy faithful mercies crown.
Jesus, thou art all compassion, pure, unbounded love thou art;
visit us with thy salvation, enter ev'ry trembling heart.

Breathe, oh, breathe thy loving Spirit into ev'ry troubled breast;
let us all in thee inherit; let us find thy promised rest.
Take away the love of sinning; Alpha and Omega be;
end of faith, as its beginning, set our hearts at liberty.

Come, Almighty, to deliver; let us all thy life receive;
suddenly return, and never, nevermore thy temples leave.
Thee we would be always blessing, serve thee as thy hosts above,
pray, and praise thee without ceasing, glory in thy perfect love.

Finish then thy new creation, pure and spotless let us be;
let us see thy great salvation perfectly restored in thee!
Changed from glory into glory, till in heav'n we take our place,
till we cast our crowns before thee, lost in wonder, love, and praise!

Text: Charles Wesley, 1707-1788

LEARNING THE STORY

After participants read the hymn background, talk about information they found meaningful or inspiring.

Look through your hymnal's index listing the sources of hymns to discover other familiar hymns by Charles Wesley.

(5 minutes)

The hymn

The last of 18 children, Charles Wesley was born in Lincolnshire, England, in 1707. Educated at Oxford he became one of the Oxford Methodists, led by his brother John Wesley, known as the founder of Methodism. After ordination in 1735, they traveled to America to work as missionaries in Georgia. During their voyage, they were deeply influenced by the enthusiastic singing of a group of Moravians.

Assurance of God's divine love is a common thread woven through the 6,500 hymns he wrote. In 1738 he returned to England and joined his brother as an itinerant preacher. Hymn singing as an ally to preaching became a trademark of the Wesleys, who published 56 collections of hymns in 53 years. Charles died in 1788.

This hymn was inspired by a popular song, "Fairest isle, all isles excelling," by John Dryden, and was first published in 1747 in *Hymns for those that Seek, and those that have Redemption.*

The tune

HYFRYDOL—"good cheer"—was composed by Rowland Prichard, who was born in North Wales in 1811 and died in 1887. He was named after his grandfather, Rowland Huw, a famous bard. HYFRYDOL was published in his *Cyfaill y Cantorion* (1844). Spanning only six notes in the musical scale the tune has become one of the most beloved in the repertory.

OUR STORY

What do you remember about the first time you heard this hymn?

What personal memories do you associate with this hymn?

What does this hymn say to you?

You may need to adapt these questions for the participants in your group. Ask them to record their responses and then share their stories. *(10 minutes)*

THE BIBLICAL STORY

Invite participants to find the passages in their Bibles and record their responses to the questions.

Breathe, oh, breathe thy loving Spirit Into ev'ry troubled breast
John 20:19-23

When have you experienced the breath of Jesus within you?

Come, Almighty
Matthew 24:30

The hymn is a prayer to Jesus, yet Almighty is usually ascribed to God. Do you think of Jesus as Almighty? In what ways?

. . . to deliver
Matthew 1:21

In what ways have you experienced Jesus as deliverer? From what do you need continuing deliverance?

Let us all thy life receive
2 Corinthians 5:17

What is the life we receive?

evermore thy temples leave
John 14:23

*What are the temples Jesus inhabits? Describe
our experiences of "being the temple." What
other biblical passages talk about the body as a
temple?*

Determine if your
group would prefer
to:
◆ read and respond
to all passages and
questions before
talking
◆ read, respond,
and discuss one
passage at a time
(20 minutes)

ay, and praise thee without ceasing
1 Thessalonians 5:16-19

*How do you pray without ceasing in a busy
schedule?*

*What connection do you discover between prayer
and praise?*

anged from glory into glory
2 Corinthians 3:18

*In a society that values youth, how can you
"change from glory into glory" as you grow
older?*

LIVING THE STORY

Invite participants to reflect for a few moments on today's conversation, and then respond to the questions. It is important to share responses to these questions so your group can offer prayer support for each other throughout the next week.

Take a few minutes to talk about future studies your group might want to pursue.

Close by singing, "Love Divine, All Loves Excelling," or you may wish to sing all five hymns from *Hymns on Prayer.*

(10 minutes)

What does this hymn say to you at this time in your life?

How does it affect the way you live each day?

How does this hymn speak to your prayer life?

Love divine, joy of heaven,
  fill us with your love divine.
Fix in us thy humble dwelling;
  nevermore thy temples leave.
Thank you for your servants—
  the poets and musicians—
  who bless your church with their gifts.
Listen now to the hearts and minds of your people
Silence for reflection.
In your holy name we pray. Amen

RESOURCES

ompact Discs

St. Olaf Choir: Great Hymns of Faith ("What a Friend We Have in
sus," track 14; "Love Divine, All Loves Excelling," track 19). The St.
laf Choir; Anton Armstrong, conductor. To order, call 507-646-3646 or
mail music@stolaf.edu

ano Arrangements

A Global Piano Tour ("What a Friend We Have in Jesus"), Mark Sedio.
igsburg Fortress, Publishers (ISBN 0-8006-5819-1). To order, call 1-800-
8-4648 or go to www.augsburgfortress.org/store

From the Heart: Sacred Piano Stories ("What a Friend We Have in
sus"), Pam Gervais. Augsburg Fortress, Publishers (ISBN 0-8006-5948-
. To order, call 1-800-328-4648 or go to www.augsburgfortress.org/store

*Let it Rip! At the Piano: Congregational Song Accompaniments for
ano* ("What a Friend We Have in Jesus," "Love Divine, All Loves
celling"). Augsburg Fortress, Publishers (ISBN 0-8006-5906-6). To
der, call 1-800-328-4648 or go to www.augsburgfortress.org/store